hot mud poems

kill poet press
Los Angeles

hot mud poems

ISBN 978-0-6151-3506-9

kill poet books are available at bulk discount rates for educational purposes.

kill poet press
www.killpoet.com
info@killpoet.com or contact the author directly at alveraz1@yahoo.com

Printed in the Unites States of America

HOT
MUD
POEMS

ALVERAZ RICARDEZ

ILLUSTRATIONS BY
JOSHUA RHODES

kill poet press
Los Angeles

various poems first published in:

pemmican

chronogram

softblow

miPOesias

defenestration

shouted whisper

down in the dirt

kill poet

language and culture

level

AVQ

for erin, parker & carson

Contents

Introduction

My wife and I decided that I would stay home with the boys over the summer. I'm a screenwriter by trade and typing scripts while chasing around the rascals was not in the cards. I needed to keep the juices flowing but at a condensed rate.

So I chose to write poems between diaper changes and romps in the park. This book was the outcome. A small portion of this verse is autobiographical. The rest covers the people I know and the people in my dreams.

I hope you enjoy it as much as I have.

In arms,
Alveraz Ricardez

four suburban churros

my rusted fam-packed volvo shakes
between crushed oil and a patriot sun

the kids; rubber-banded jumping beans
the wife drives like a thawing chihuahua

i cut a deal with the bad breath of traffic,
my eyes roll back; a slack-jawed, wet steak

rare and slow cooked, i'm sure to be
well-done by san diego and jerky by tijuana

just because you say what

spiced bellies and sugared hips
after ten years of shared sheets
we finally taste like each other

retired in red

on the lawn between
soft fallen lemons
and fresh vined lattice
was the onion breathed
spaniard and his lunatic cat

he wept for the children
painted into his fields of
wheat and bananas

he settled the parents
in mulch along the rim
of his easel

he dreamt the birth
of fresh stalk would rise
against land lords and
propagate these fields
into milled flour

they would feed
the lucid workers
and forgiven bourgeois

he was the new savior
and weathered nemesis
of failed autocracy

he would finally kiss
the sewed soil of youth
and tango with his ancestors:
they would rise, damn it, rise!

and below the storm

his lunatic cat pawed
at the coagulated paint
bone dry brushes
and unkempt beard

he knew the old man
cried from his onion sandwich
and by dusk there would
only be an empty canvas
soft fallen lemons, and fresh vined lattice

nutshells

on my way across
the park today
two elderly asian women
leaped from behind a tree

they were sword fighting

this is not a metaphor
just old ladies that
mastered the big secret:

without shackle
time or tomorrow

sign here

the banter of war and burnt mellows
dropped like dead cadets when richie said
I don't know whether to fight or play chess

sealed berries

do you remember the stink of ripe melon on my lips
and the dance of pioneer i played on your back?

you tongued the cherried pimples below
my left shoulder and hummed a tune of insurrection

we dressed in skyline and bathed in sinuous cum
(this was the wake of champions unbound)

a whole new direction of filth and song
a whole new direction of obscene abandon

we giggled at the sound of bullhorns
and planted soft kisses on each bullet

the corners of our room soaked in defense
the windows nailed shut; our bed wet and warm

we painted the ceiling with urine and played
patty cake for seven hours straight

we climaxed to the rattle of flames set by pigs
and we laughed at their naked portly bodies

these were the final moments of clarity and spring
before the lock of metal cages and tomorrow's noose

for my bride

why touch the pen to paper
when the deep white
reminds me of you
the quiet times

we compare the
rhythm of our bellies
i slow mine down
to be more like you

drunken toes gather
under a silk pub
and drift into sweat
by our raft of hum

my fingers rest in the hollow
just behind your ankle
not a word but we know
this is the devil's playground

the billow of our breath
dance between us
the yawn of two giants
in love

daddy was a sailor

when I was two he forced me
to cross through a spider web in the door frame
one year later he would leave my mother

post-kaboom

Upon arrival the empathetic social workers from
surviving countries applied Vapo-Rub under their noses.
They sterilized scalpels and politely shook hands.

One worker found the head of Rumsfeld with thousands
of sturgeon floating in a radiated fish farm outside of Topeka.

At a truck stop in New Jersey they found the scorched carcass
of Mickey Mouse on the bathroom floor. His white gloves
smartly preserved between his ass cheeks.

They stumbled across a field of popcorn babies outside of
Wichita Falls. In Los Angeles, a hotel lobby of leather was
seared to naked rock stars, with uncompromised big hair.

Inside the Pentagon's walk-in closet were 500 unfortunate
businessmen, and on the roof; the slow boiled remains
of every congressional wife, covered in, what could only
be described as designer cotton.

One worker scratched at his chin from behind a rusted shack in
Orlando; *Hey, fellas, is this the body of an Oscar winner or a*
school teacher?

With soda can grabbers they plucked the president's family from
an apple tree in Vermont and placed them in left over zip lock
bags; the ones with the patented fresh seal.

Each social worker shared an uncomfortable but understood glance of agreement. They quietly removed their gloves and deemed the land uninhabitable.

Later the United States would be systematically chiseled off into the ocean. And the tales of what the social workers found would become legendary folk-lore, whispered to children before they went to sleep.

city kill and the headdress

wet bark and oak leaves stick
to my crotch after a campfire
fuck with the wife

in our tent we suck beer farts
and tickle our nipples
for levity

the moon, a god damn liar
slips in whitman's mud
before my eyes can adjust

one smoke and a final
dance with the indians before
temporary death

later I would lose my wedding
ring in the river and hate that trip
forever

surviving september

september is thick like sternum
and with every bottled dawn
she anchors to my foreskin

we will miss the laughs
but her visit this time round
will be the end of our affair

we buckle to our knees on my
bathroom floor and flush
twenty years from her pores

she will fall back into quarters
with her siblings, and our rind will
separate into duality and journals

asking for much

I want to know Greek names and spread them around like
mayonnaise. I want to say those names between smart adjectives
when I know the other person is bored with me.

Why did I leave college knowing I would end up an alcoholic
artist, with a hungry daughter, and a wife that was fooled into me?

Now that I am sober I want to know a lot of things, and I hope that
no one finds out that I was lying the whole time; that I am a stupid
man, with a lot to learn. Only now have my bones decided to
harden.

I am 61 years old and I want to know why.

sleeping bag

you never knew I spent years following the lines in your hands,
each night a new journey while you slept

the hot air in this desert reminds me of your palms,
and I miss your fingers right now

bread and wine

she stinks like patchouli
her pit hair's a back alley twist

she knows i'm greased for pound
ready for molded pew

we crack teeth against sticky walls
a good ten chokes before communion

the mix of my junk against her ass
shakes the last bit of saint from spine

we bite down for fuck and mercy
we roll with the sound of religious freedom

the long road

helen chadwick and her husband harold
won the sunday night bridge game

they squandered their winnings on two
hot plates of liver, hash and okra

on the way home from the diner
harold left his wife a pleasant surprise

he removed his weathered derby and laid
his head in her lap

he then winked at his blushing bride
and drifted off for the last time

me hungry

carson sleeps with a wooden tiger
and i worry he will wake with a bruise
and blame india for sending such
a troublesome beast to sleep with

season under soil

she will tie knots in the victory
and roll it from her new
american window

she will wrench the apathy from
dried husks and bleed it over
white history books

the damp of colonized beards
will be cut with rusted arrow
dried with campaign of awake

iron toothpicks from capitol pillars
for paint dips on fresh wooden walls
slow like cigar and native dance

the roots will be cared for
the surplus accounted for
and the spring mortar sewed

sword fallen campfire songs
chase the last ember of empire
and saturated banks

she will ride the cobbled streets
on her bicycle and wave the salty
quilted flag of fist and harmony

grumpy zazen

a clear sign of cushion neglect
arrived just below my nose
above my browned gums
like an old pouting vagina

i know it's time to get
back on that black cloud
and wipe the dust
from the three jewels

i can only hope the bowl
still rings like i remember;
that the bodhisattvas still
tickle my toes in half lotus

hope the hot steam of balls
after twenty minutes inside
still flushes the nostril
and rids me of duality

maybe the drop of lids into
almond slivers and the warm
penis thumb-tip touches
will encourage the open door

can i settle down when i forget
my breath-count, fart, giggle
or hum that one song
by twisted sister?

the need to get busy sitting
counters the balance anyway
and i find plenty more excuses
to play with my cat instead

chavez still smelled sulfer

there is no spring, butter or lilacs in political poetry
only elbowed metal and diseased intangibles
the pigs own lipstick slides to mud
when faced with a pen of two parties

past the yellow gate

there is a secluded area of painted gorge
where billy goats make love under the sun

my crew voted to strip naked
and see what these goats were made of

the only sound was rock threaded wind
when fifteen naked boys met fifteen horny goats

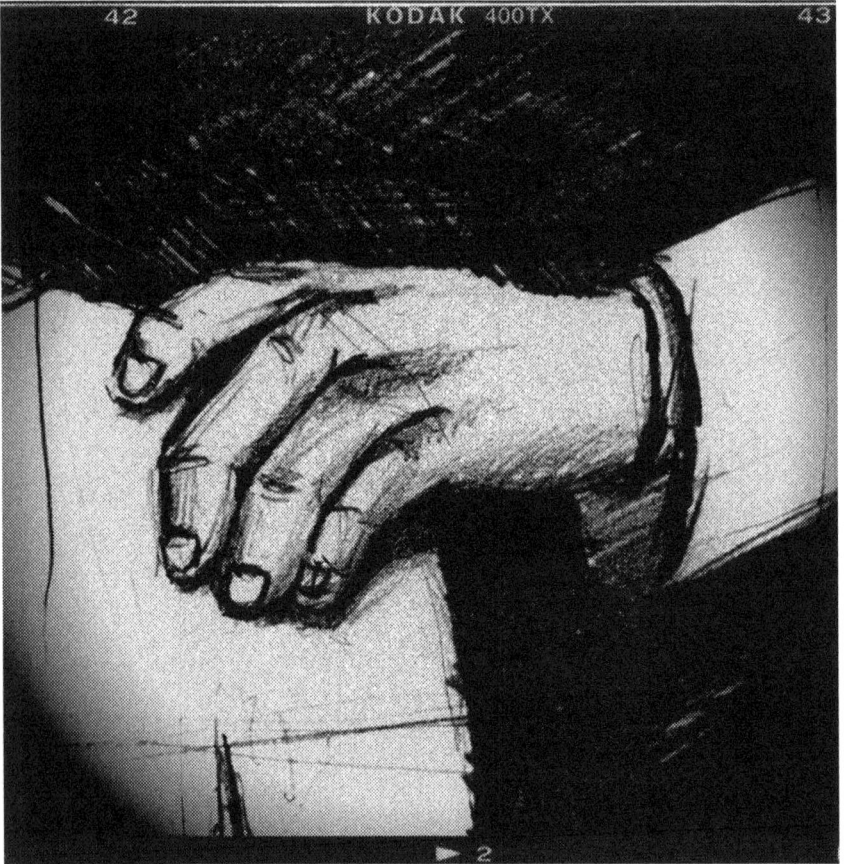

porque llama queso queso?

I was approached by a Latino hero of mine and asked if I spoke Spanish. My breath being lost, I shook my head. He placed his hand on my shoulder, looked me square in the eyes and said,

So you are a Mexican't.

He laughed and walked off.
I had been comfortably marginalized by a Chicano warrior for being a half breed, and I was once again last to be picked in dodge ball.

breaking up with nature

below my inhale the fig tree
yields at the smell of candied brothels
and moist flower-bed pores

i press my ear against her trunk
and listen to the hours of rustled nuts
and the tally of suited squirrels

both in unison
both under pressure
both at my leisure

below my exhale
the wind snorts
and pisses in my mouth

with each trail down my chin
another fig atrophies under
the wake of pigeon shit

we both decide
the best measure
is a clean break

we both decide
to stop breathing
at the same time

bunny slippers

caught on the devil's toilet
swollen eyes and spitting fire
between the blinds

you

in

my

cross-hairs

like a wet sore
a hot diaper in my beer

get out from under
my fingernails

every
morning
with
that
fucking
lawnmower

I'm double fisting this time
my cock and a blade
let me grab my robe

and set another
plate
for
breakfast

hot dung

I'm watching National Geographic
and there's this giant elephant
in some rural Indian village
striking fear into the locals.

He's already killed thirty of them.
This guy says the elephant knocks
on doors with his foot,
waits for you to answer
then snatches you with his trunk.

He prays to Ganesh this never
happens to him.

So I swallow a warm shot
of tequila and go
knock on my neighbors door
(the one with the lawnmower).

fistful of chips

just trying to find
a little corner of the world;
somewhere for you
and i to share a beer.

right here.
this is cool.
an underpass.
smells like shit
and urine;
perfect.

got an angle both ways for the cops.
i'll open yours, then mine.
i want you to talk to me right now,
more than ever.

not many people knew
it ain't fun getting
blackjack on every hand,
but you did.

hi-ho silver

showers of antiquated saddles
flood the pastures of my cowboy dreams

my pine oiled squaw leaps onto me
her pussy warms the small of my back

a blur of orange war paint splashes
our browning as we race to shelter

we hide under the overgrown noodle tree
and build a fire with soldier bones

you are now a grasshopper with bow
and tsk, tsk, tsk, for *smash you*

my heel rises over your antennae
as you weep for new buffalo

and like a sucker I build a tepee from the
antiquated saddles of my cowboy dreams

another blessed morning with thick sleep
in my eyes; harnessed to my wife's ass

born without birth

listen to the space
just below my navel
where the vine grows
and the whispers settle

where moments are implied
and death is due process

where everything is now
and life is nothing more
than this

jimmy was her bitch

the sweat of two
bare chested pogo sticks
dance from yard to yard
in the summer of '83

connected by pale skin and tenuous frames
twins by birth, status by incident;
my sister, the princess acute
and i, the duke of dumb

we turn into my shed skin,
the alley of jimmy dugan;
mustard teeth and pinball eyes:
he busted my skull with a horseshoe

i'm a puddle of blood;
my sister bites through her lip;
and in a blur of chick power
little jimmy shits his pants

my sister fucking ruled

the feet of immigrants

Let them bathe in my sweat, feed on my muscle;
clip my nails for flint, burn my legs for warmth.
Let them sleep in my belly, wake with my soul;
cull my hide for shade, drain my urine for fence.

Give my heart for the toll road, when they arrive;
my nose for the swine, my palate for freedom.
Give my voice to stand on, when they arrive;
my eyes for the truth, my ears for the lies.

pre-heat

my country has baked itself into the corner of a cookie sheet
and like all congested pastries under-fire, it rolls over onto
the oven floor, and smokes me out of my own home
and now, I'm homeless.

and I don't even like pastries.

for my geeshie wiley

stumble out for another interview
the a.m. blonde says 110 by noon
but she
just
wants
me
that
way

a little air between
armpits and nuts

should've topped the gut
and aired the tank
but I know my geeshie steel
and she don't take
that kinda fuel
(what's with not smoking
at the pump anyway)

the on-ramp of lost veterans
with empty buckets and
tyrone's body-shop chariot
his ball-breaking thumps
and broken window rollers

i'm at my maker's gate
flash of a hamster's chest
rising, falling
no matter how hard
i yell to push that wheel

same

pace

every

time

so i can
forgive these fuckers
my rearview says my brow
sunk further than this morning

but that was ten minutes ago
(4pm)

i angle it at my cock
and turn the radio to rome
take the last drag
and adjust my posture
for the limo next to me
(you never know)

and i finally
see
the
hold
up

no shit
a kitchen table
on all fours

in

the

fast

lane

eyes burn from the savvy getty glare
but i can see the breakfast dead
wrapped around oak
like dead squirrels

poppa and his corncob
little pink panties
and her hidden crush
jimmy toad-in-pocket
either lickin lips at
the pork chops
or daddy's prize

how do they do it
mid-405 congestion
chewing at the smog and guts
like i do
in the
best
of
my
dreams

turns out my padres
are the tallest midget this year
and i'm okay with that

rack me

summer poem

truckers yank chords at me
and chicks flash their tits
but that's the trick ain't it;
drive a hundred, jerk-off
and not crash

maybe I should call mom
maybe play with the kids
maybe I should pull over
and pick-up needlepoint.

death of birthday boy

Exhaust filled my nostrils, or was it his Old Spice?
A whirlwind of flannel and denim; frail in a wooden box
on cracked wheels, I was tethered to his iron horse:
a punished sailor trailing my captain by dingy.
Beneath that stoic beard was my father;
and coiled in this cart, his ten year old son.

His hand lifted; a sign to set anchor.
In the thick of a redwood he spotted our prey.
The ocean of foliage knelt before him;
lip curled, brow furrowed, he was man, I was soft.

I followed his finger to a high branch.
A caramel-coated squirrel stretched under shade.
He winked, I smiled; my time had come. Crosshairs set,
he whispered, fire. I swallowed hard, set my heels.
I don't remember pulling the trigger--
or the sound of gunfire.

I only remember screams from the redwood above.
The bullets flew; her presence grew louder;
more shots would temper her cries
and earn his love.

She held on by a nail, her honeyed coat
soaked red as my eyes. The final shot silenced her;
The pregnant squirrel that lay at our feet
now bigger than my father.

little babushka

park your cab
hot trash
and alley grope
sessions fade

whisper another
tale of lenin
to top this
patriot off

slip under
your dash
a smelly
manifesto
seal the windows
hit the heater
and hot box
for extra slide

chew my lip
peel your ass
from the
leather

for

balance

and

country

I tongue
your pit hair
into cherry stems
our thumbs
disappear
and we laugh
for hours

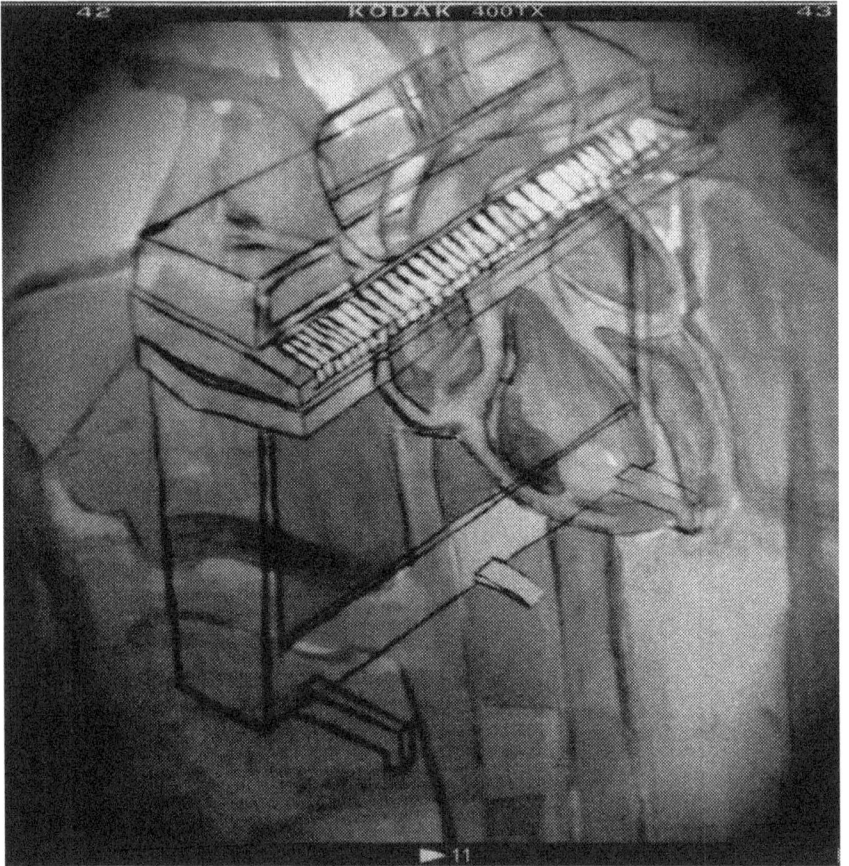

better this way

(   )   ,   ;
   ,   ,   :
            ,   ,

         ,   ,   ;
,   ;   !

pow wow by proxy

bear loudreaux was a french indian gun fighter
wrapped in a cultural stereotype
for every step he took off high ground
he landed with much more than intended

nods from prospectors and shallow greased
trappers poured from each saloon at his feet
the mighty red of cheyenne and the
gristled chin of jerkied warriors cemented
his spine and liquored his eyes

every dead man was another day he would
be forced to live

he knew the consequence of his rifle
and the red skin under his fathered savvy
but there was more to this under the hide of legend

a woman by campfire waits for his return in
a small ravine bellied under the yukon valley
she would sing his song before the crack of her neck
and fist the balls of white men
in the name of her sweet bear loudreaux

divorce

when I clicked enter
a message appeared

your browser sent a request
that this server could not understand

my cat and I wept for hours;
the years of trust and sacrifice
between browser and server;

suddenly, and without warning,
broken into fragments
over a simple misunderstanding

brad

I was convinced that cinema was in ruin,
and that my next script would be gold

I opened three red envelopes
The Squid & The Whale
Proof
Me and You & Everyone We Know

I was convinced that cinema was saved,
and that my next script would be shit

free shuck

sit up here little boy
                          let's paint   a picture
together

something porous
               maybe
                     like dried sea sponge

                       we can dance   naked
in white wash
and
  kick up   devil rays

let's grab a snow cone
and   see what's on the
                        radio
something inside that static feels   purple

     right?

when we tangle our ankles
                over
                  the
                    boardwalk
there's more
         this
           than
             that
and it's all   plaid   peanuts from here
on

we catch that corner look from our eyes

61

left   center
of sun

that's the

sand jig my boy,   that's the   sand jig

and there's a whole lotta soda
                                          pop
and jelly beans this time out

and   halleluha for baked toes and   brisk whiskers   on
fishing boats

haroooga! haroooga!
and   scallyboodaloooo!

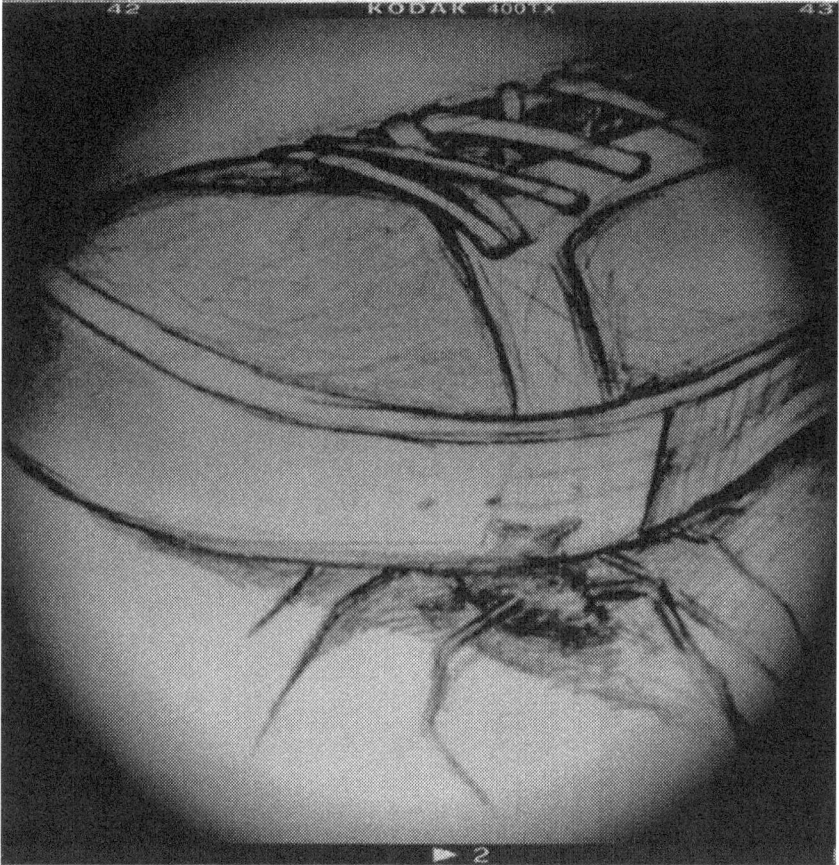

maybe tomorrow

only when I'm drunk do I realize
there's more to write about than being drunk,
but I'm drunk, so

prime time

they removed the wire handles
from chinese take-out boxes
for microwave ease

a cool smile on my cat's face;
another reason to stay in bed
and pick crumbs from my belly hair

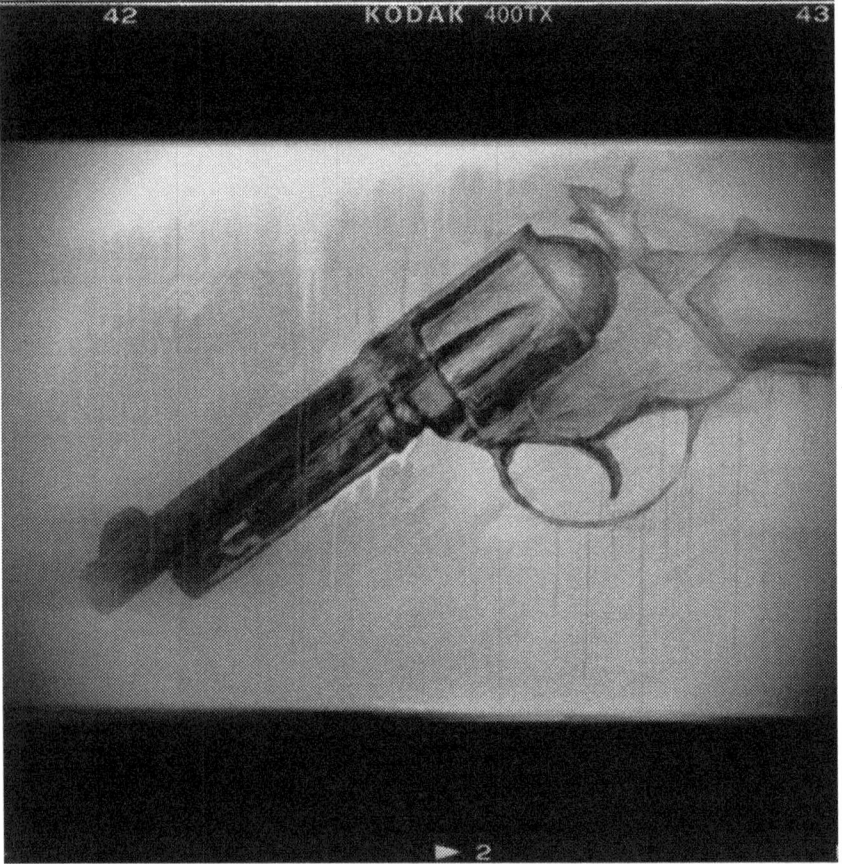

behind you

five of us climbed a desert cliff to capture gunfire;
we had ten minutes before the sand-wall of god
would slam damn upon us

the camera rolled and we took hold;
on the first gunshot the storm lifted us into palm
and placed us into the ravine

we could not speak or see through the howl
but our shared smile confirmed
our love for independent film

pomegranate tree

we chased catfish
like careless hooligans

if I was older I would
have noticed the liver spots

if I was older I would have
asked you to sit with me and cry

I would have asked you to rest those
calloused hands and breathe out
for once in your life

the cement tango

wet sneakers on motel-mud cushion her broken toes

ant-flowers bloom on both red-hilled arms

she is reckless with god and

spits fire after

every

sip

of

sin

taste of pimp knuckles and rope scrub the princess

from beneath her hide, a daily service of vagabond cum

back alley profits hum ballads of clean sheets and

a little town not

too

far

from

here

sickness steams from rot-gut and the child inside
hot trash and sticky hips devil under man-hole
his moist whisper by sewer's edge:
take my hand

and

dance

with

me

to power

plucked by wingless muscled crows
this is the birthplace of complex cotton

the new century of scrubbed toenails
and fenced in polymers

where pickled capillaries and sticky cheeks
trade up models for swollen brown skies

vines of idle angels bored behind churches
chew ample yellow big macs and warm apostle jam

where sons of suited wrinkles mount
wet uniform imports in soap-boxed pine

but there is comfort with each gasp
the tick, tick, tick of well placed absolutes

rain on corrugated awnings reminds me of zapata
but the smell of giant thumb stretches for days

the scream of fat kids on rusted bicycles
trumpets from the heavens

and we know that christ has returned
just like he said he would

off the wall

we pulled the crate of vinyl from the closet;
somewhere between drive like jehu
and memphis minnie was
michael jackson's off the wall

we foiled the windows, lit candles
and danced till the wicks ran out;
michael smoothed it in the first verse:

when the world is on your shoulder
gotta straighten up your act and boogie down
if you can't hang with the feeling
then there ain't no room for you in this part of town
cause we're the party people night and day
livin' crazy that's the only way

dear lady friend

your bull has a bloody nose
how the hell do you plan to
revise such a poem

do not finger my asshole
and whisper in my ear
do not nibble my nipples
and share wound with me

this is not what it should be
and you damn well know it

a poem with the taste of brine:
the smell of game
the sound of paper cut
the touch of cancer

from a tree hacked toothpick
you settle a bet between your teeth
and now you have the nerve
to cry from the pain

you are the naked dictator of
shitty verse and you disgust me

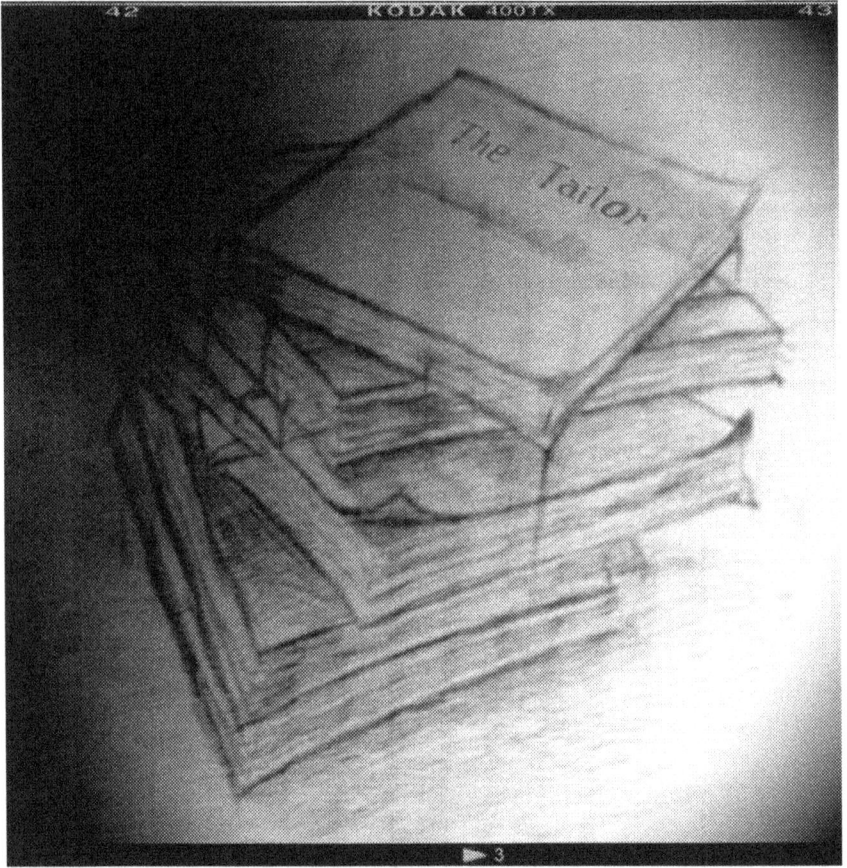

i slept in church

god is pissed with act three
and ocotillo has lost it's touch

I'm convinced he found a script
lying around base camp

he has surely decided to
end me before I end this film

pop's kitchen and the pea pardon

This man of gristle and iron sat across from me,
now just a pile of uneven mud. His hair caked
back with pomade thick as Pennzoil;
his cracked brow furrowed like bad pottery.

I got a ten-spot says you can't bust those chops
with a jackhammer. He cleared his throat;
an instant reveille.

Holding that fork between his pudgy taters
struck a funny bone. An unconscious hum
of Hank Williams edged from his leather lips
like a broke jukebox.

He poked at it; scratched his sandstone cheeks,
and one-eyed the last thing on his plate.
Intrigued by a natural frown gone deeper; I smile.

I tongue the last bit of squash from my teeth,
and stop in my tracks. Ever see a giant
struggle with a pea? I have, and it was the first time
in my life I felt sorry for the old bastard.

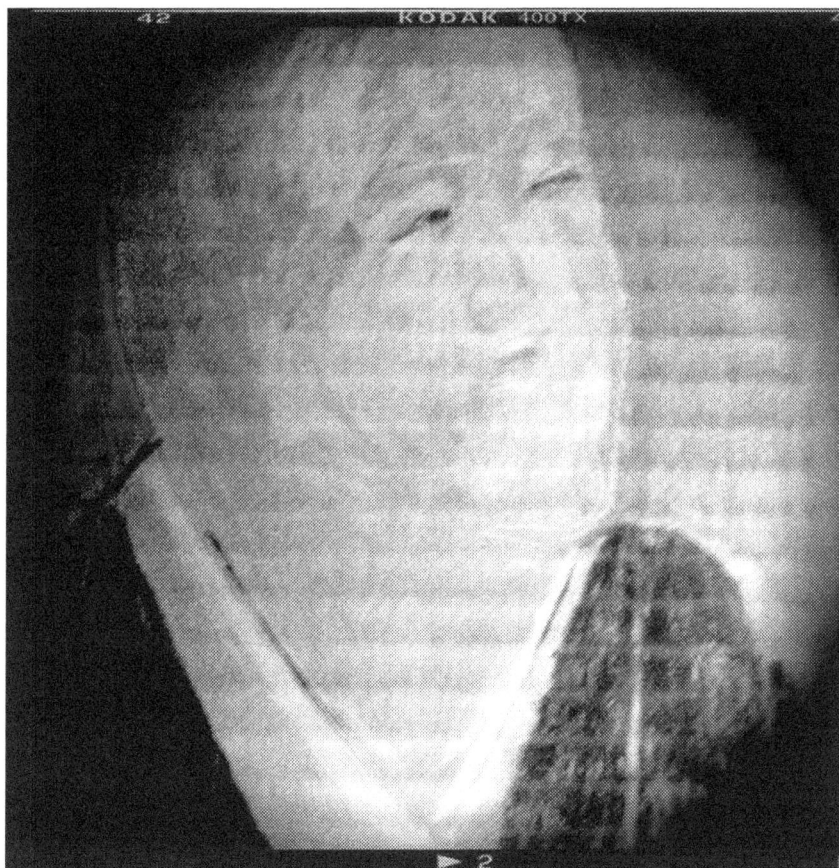

bubblegum tacks

while in little league I had a poster
of tony gwynn over my bed
as a teenage leftist; debs
as a screenwriter; arriaga
as a buddhist; dogen
now a poet; tony gwynn

polar bear hunter

and fragment   dream
                whisper several chapters by cornelius
my one   black friend
he is forever   polar bear

                        hunter

with wild
roots and afro
strength of
                        men I wanted be
                but fail lack of will power and
poor politic understand
                        he was
            giant
silverback hero
his shards in sleep was   me to
wake from
and his hurdled by street knowledge
known to topple
                government

he say

we leaps from burrowed
                                burn
                                    taxi
we land on iceberg
cornelius with spectacles and I wit

naked eye like
wit no will at all

like I done been
suckered already

        before
we even   started

we right in front of the man
and he got
        ice chips

      cause we
          parched and he
              with honeyed voice and
                    red tie likes the way
                          we smell
my cornelius
laugh a boulevard like red star

            to guide us
              he digs into
                snow

says

              the fuck we need
           yo chips fo, mother fucker?

I swallow and reach for   the
ice chips

because   it   was   easier
and
cornelius   always   did
things
the
      hard

way

he was
hydrated and I was
still

parched   but warm by
his giant
black hand
he smile and place his
spectacles on my eyes
I spot the red tie now knotted on polar bear and
my slickened
seal hair

and cornelius
speared him before I was another prisoner of
ice chips

highway hooker and the desert motel

let me leap
off your chin
and land within
your hips

I will dance
on your breath
paint fire
across your
wrists

when I tire
I will kill
between
your bosom
and your toes

south of angels
north of sin
your humble
vagabond

the common denominator

belly up in some desert i'd drink the blood that's made a river into my mouth but i think salt makes you more thirsty or is that ocean water my buddy hovers over me like an angel sweat drips from his hard hat halo into my mouth is he giving me shade his lips move like worms on hot cement there ain't nothing coming out i've seen that look before maybe in a movie the low hum is kinda warm from my ear it soaks the sand under my head i feel like i'm back in a jacuzzi with my girlfriend the one we used to sneak into remember that one outside mr. jenkins building i notice that word he's saying he must of heard me mention the jacuzzi or something another look i recognize but that's the one my dad had in his eye when me and momma watched him get beat up by my grandpa the flyers drop from the sky like butterflies around my buddies head must be warning the locals to get out of here guess it's time to go how did i get here how did i get here how did i get here how did i get here why did i get here why did i didn't choose this but it was for a cause i'm sure of it right right right just tell me right he nods but i think he's lying to me why am i still laying here why is he brushing my hair back like that it does feel kinda good but i don't feel it anywhere so where is the good at i can see the good right there somewhere between the tip of both our noses i think it's time to go there and swim in the good he smiles back so i guess he knows i'm okay now and it's just my turn to skip to the end of the book goodbye buddy

in her prime

she spit shined
her cock-skin belt

soaked heaven
with tampons

raped nature
and fired the sun

nartz

the empty between your toes
reminds me of twisted boulevard

the lamps we light above;
the stink we find beneath

we are the *comandante* of fuck;
we are the *capitan* of poem

we know the heavy of anchor
there is no stuck, there is no doubt

there is no pilot, no bank of trust
no count of minute, no hot mud

there is only stitched hide
and buttered cool with that

we tongue boiled embers
like we lick salted rolls

you balance god with
rock oiled pussy

and we are
the marriage of panic

cover me

pop the top
grab your gun
this fucker is taking off

drop some freedom
from the belly of giants
gas up the fist of god

polish that barrel
and knuckle your balls
thunder guts for glory

hammer your chin
and toughen that skin
so you know you're still alive

under belly

he was the remains
of boiled down gold
and difficult times

one of twelve sons
and a milked mother-
no one really wanted

spread over leather
he was a salted dish
of brine and butter

fishing with fidel

barrels of dead revolutionaries line our alley
like tomcats waiting for the next heat

the con of thrift store thespians:
we're all born without kneecaps, why bother?

my coffee cools under
walnut eyelids from the temporary shock

god plays banjo

she gonna find
that religion

weave it into
a basket of man

something fierce
but bonny like

she melts by the river
and fingers it raw

but they aint no
one comin this time

one eye open
for jesus

one eye open
for panic

she say she got
bittered breath

for that pound
of humble steak

but the mayo
thicks her lips

her steam panties
scream boredom

tired of man whistle
and god sweat

she maybe got one day left
she maybe got two

two boys find religion

two dress her in wine with hands of gristle and bone
electric pussy and fine cuts of paled thigh brings
heathen breath; the new fire before christ

two calloused heads of sweet corn babies
slide into heaven and hell with the force
of hammers into a sticky glaze

two fingers meet at her last whole of need
three guttural bellows from a pair of monkeys
and a gray haired mother of god

two piles of twisted tendon and ashed volcanos
find shelter in weathered skin and cracked lips
a new day of manhood, with a slice of apple pie

turbans and tacos

CNN warns of chemical weapons
so i close my window

the next commercial is for
economical A/C units

its hot in here
so i dial the number

the guy on the phone
sounds middle eastern

i wonder if he knows
he's in the ironic zone

maybe i should smell
his ass through my cage

but he might have
the bird-flu

i ask if shots
are included

he plays dumb
then giggles

we break wind
share a toast

and tickle each other's
balls in peace

94

garbage

My lip curls inside the upc hot box of 7-11.
I stand at the beer cooler and wonder where
this blue phlegm on my chin came from.

I assume it's the berry freeze Slurpee I chugged to
cushion the blow of my twisted gut.
A guy with a red smock and the smell of my father
says I gotta close the cooler door.

I spittle a few phrases like military-industrial complex,
Hemingway hacks and the decline of Slurpee flavors;
he soldier's back that I've been there for an hour.

Sure enough the open door is frosted over.
I reach into my pants for confirmation and
sure enough my penis is the size of a june bug.
I nod and tip my Padres cap, Eastwood like.

I ask him if he can grab the beer for me.
He says something in between verbs like
cops, drunk, and bum.

I belt him across his terrorist lips
and sing my favorite going to jail song;
the one by Celine Dion, so I remember
how shitty the rest of my morning is going to be.

pull the blinds

behind the building of suits
two vaginas share cheap paperbacks;
whistle while they snort
giggle till they pee
one in love
one just in

four hours till the shadow dance ends
and the pimples pop into the street
four hours, four tits, two vaginas
and a barrel of angel sweat

four hours till both are forced under
the weathered american umbrella
made of porous stone

four hours till the stars and stripes
of old man jenkins and his
gum slaps, rocking chair
and shotgun spins the burnt
tune that never ends

four hours till
he wants a little pussy
himself; and they wake
under his thumb

roberto's habitual hobby

roberto hands over intellectual
credit to emaciated consumers
by raising the ninety-nine cent tags
to one dollar

he dances the grocery store jig
there will be no fools today!

he burns down la mancha with label guns
and scores hashmarks into florescent liquor aisles

he rocks the egg cooler of free economy
and pisses off the bipartisan shoppers

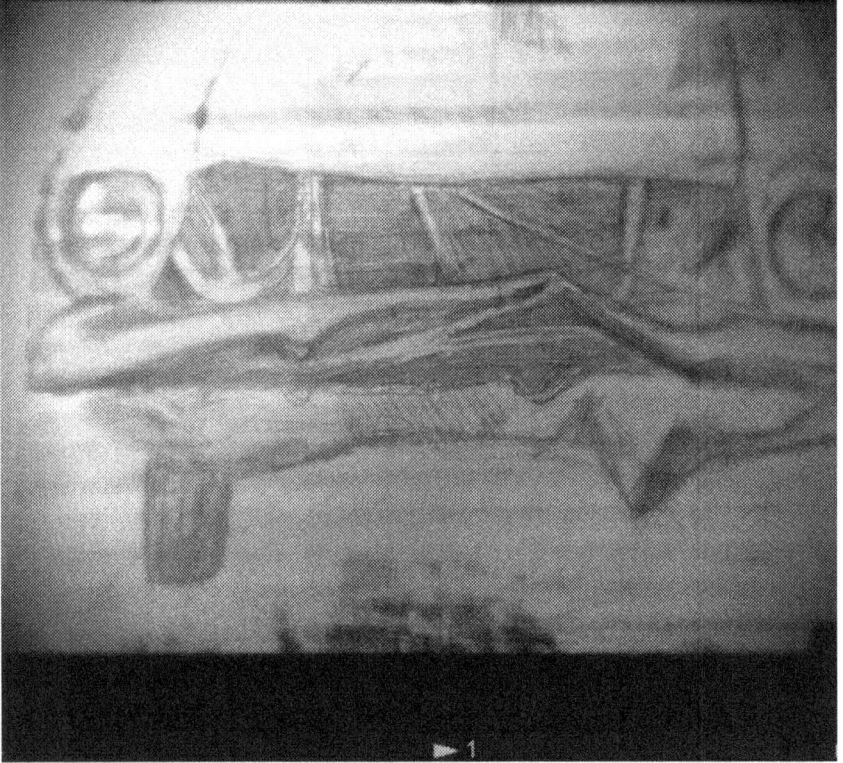

the great escape of '88

My ford was cooked and I was lost. I pulled
into the town of just swell. The ravine
of blue hair-conditioned tract homes
sucked what little smoke was left in my lung.

A swarm of spider veined Reaganites walked the root-
cracked sidewalks. I was surrounded;
and there wasn't a damn thing I could do about it.

I tempered my haste and weaseled my way
under the hood without alarming the natives.
Popped my Pabst and manned my block;
I whispered in her ear,
I'll get you through this, baby.

I focused through the glare of tea jugs
and sun spotted legs in polyester socks.

I'll be damned if that fucking poodle
wasn't as smug as its leash holding grin;
but who was I to judge.

The miles of coiled green hose on saturated lawns
twisted my gut something fierce. The sound
of pimpled larvae tugging at the teats of stepford's
caused a painful twitch in my cock.

I polished my baby just right and dropped the hood;
pounded the gas and left grease in my wake.
The zombies in my rearview were frozen in defeat;
I beat them perfect and victory was mine.

damn it

if you want me to take out the trash, just ask
i don't need the eye of aughra
like i'm a fucking gelfling
jesus

summer of scallywags

oak leaves into eye patches
twigs into mighty swords
my pearl and bronze boys
now pirates off playground shores

nut drunken sea-squirrels
and merry-go tide pools
a jungle-gym mutiny
your demise, walk the slide

from the quilted sands below
the captain takes anchor
his crew must scavenger
for cold cuts and juice

take heed while you swing
ye land-lovers be warned
these full-bellied pirates
will return once more

dumb noodles in the mirror

three leagues below my nipple
one gray hair swims against
the tide of beer sweat

he reaches shore
a rash, shaped like
my mothers thigh

with little rest and whale piss
he swims for the two coves
on each side of my head

he selects the left one
as the right has been leased
to a couple stiffs in gel

kill your ly

me and my friend
hunt unicorn poets
with our bare teeth

the sad ones that
wear black
and feel things

they forget
crotch and stink
but we remind them

i like the ones
with small tits
and big eyes

he likes the ones
with fat butts
and thick mascara

down

erin asked me not to drink this evening
and changed my poems for the rest of my life

cummings had cubism
i have my wife
(this is a good thing)

oasis

the burn from thirty-two pints
and a japanese whore
gripped his sack and twisted
like a pepper grinder
over an american steak

ask him if he heard his own
capillaries pop when he
shot snot across the room
my bet is, he could

faux plants and bullshit
paintings of red koi kicked
the vomit into full gear
each finger-dam broke
with a warm mess

fingers, he thought;
were they really that green,
or was it the florescent lighting

he smiled between heaves
remembered his mother's tuna casserole,
the crushed chips and peas;
she was a fine cook
better than the shit around here
fucking heathens

he pulled the last hair from his ass
wiped the jelly from his chin
and there she was

under a pile of sticky sheets
one last ride on the dragon
before breakfast

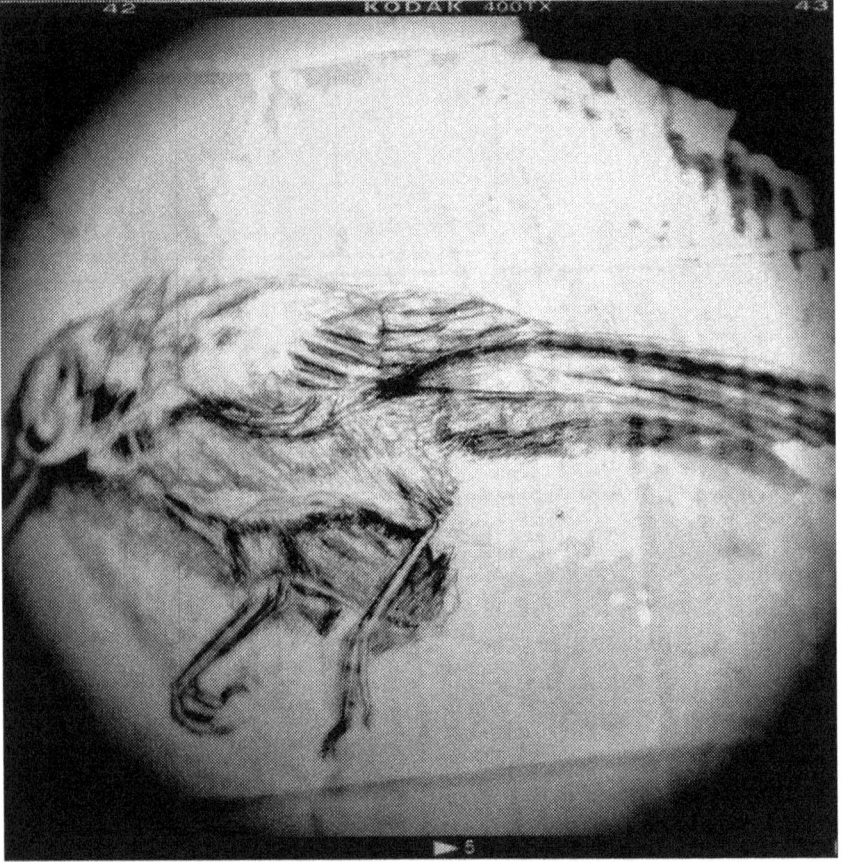

the man in tight jeans

stuck in traffic under brautigan's verse:
little prayers the size of dead birds
it cools my tongue and settles a very
bad temper

armchair pacifist

let's hold hands and forget our breath today
nibble our kite strings and fly over church
tip touch our cocks and sing songs of li ho

let's hold hands and forget our breath today
whittle bone rafts and float past the poor
stomp gutter and cover in foul taste of oil

let's hold hands and forget our breath today
spit shine our thumbs and tickle bordered ass
pick tripe from our teeth and soak blistered toes

let's hold hands and forget our breath today
glue us turkey lips and run past the war
belly flop milk to recover from george

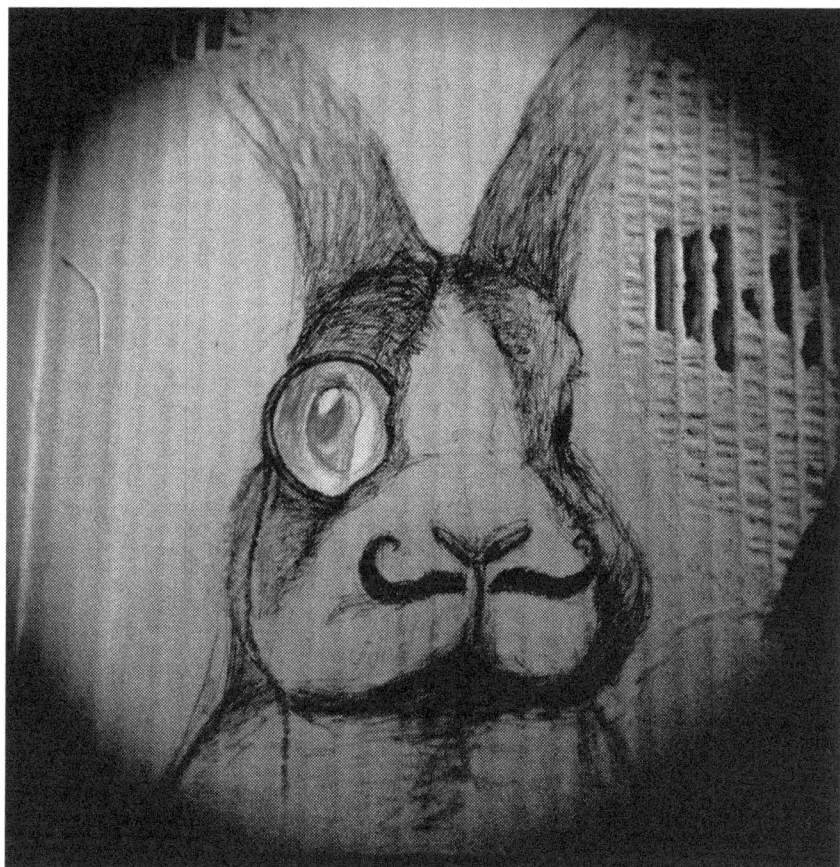

the absurd rabbit of 100 acre woods

my opinions on most provocative subjects
are relative to the time of day
and the amount of toxins in my body

there is little doubt the level of emotion
will be on a sliding scale at any given time

in the morning before tea and with a clean system
the answers will be sharp, seemingly harsh and indirect

and post-tea they will be direct, but still sharp and seemingly harsh
the clarity of my argument will have also blossomed

if provoked during work you can expect
the same results as previous to my tea,
but at a vastly higher volume

however the ratio of direct and indirect will differ in accordance
with the question, and what I may be wearing at the time,
as all opinions are mounted from my confidence
which derives from one's attire

the same applies to pre and post dinner, or any other
digestibles I suppose, with exception to alcohol
the toxin of spit I am rightly told

only after a pleasant walk or a filthy fuck
will you find my moustache waxed
and eyepiece centered

if the light is just so and the area smells of ginger
then you may be surprised to find
my opinions are quite delightful

guilt by association

my boys tube down the river right;
with a cooler of wal-mart
and natural selection

chipped cogs on a starved wheel
they get fatter by the day
stuffed blind by my own design;
a hot mud foundation.

first generation of indifference gives way
to modem monkeys with myspace pimples
your shiny tools cranked gears and patched leeks
now rusted by apathy (in my drawer)

calloused fingers lead indifferent meat
online protest by the millions
how dare my government betray me
http, backslash, backslash, colon
mydoorhasdissapeared.com

my rope of apology
before they drown reads
sorry for paying the internet bill

goof

mr. x mentions the abandon of
traditional publishing
and marketing

he speaks of a hope-margin
a place where large towns
have one local brewery
one local newspaper

some mention of arrival
with a similar community
through our writing

i lean back and wonder
if there was ever a poet
that pushed another poet
out of his chair like i will do
to mr. x

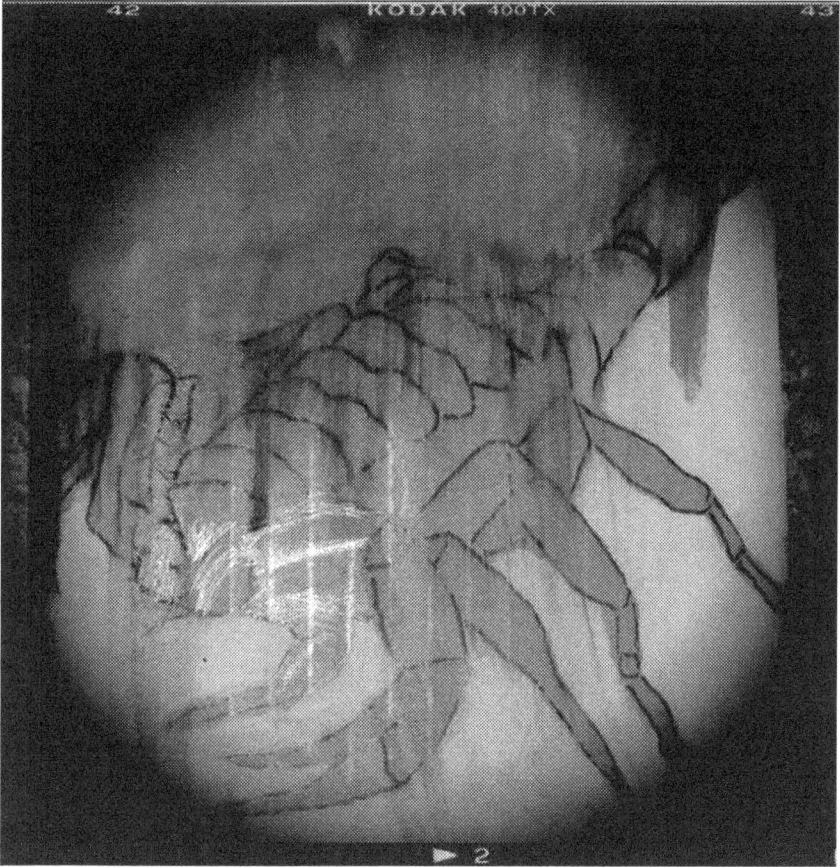

dreams of sinaloa

horseback on a clay trail in jalisco
i find two vanilla cream scorpions;
one on it's back and one in tears

i ask the sad scorpion if he knows
the way back to colima

his sun cracked voice
whispers between spittled sand
save me from being without my isabella

his eyes roll back and his arms
lift with the rise of my boot

i scoop the dead lovers into my palm
and bury them on the side of the
clay trail in jalisco

chatter

I wake to exhausted faces
and clammy skin.
Once again I have gone too far

october 13th, 2006

the big snow of buffalo arrives
with the end of my poems

the parks have closed with a twist
of locks and a swank shake of the ass

the new challenge of prose
smacks with cigar and molasses

the indoor sweat tastes of
hippie hopes for christmas

the laptop burns like a rifle barrel
her due rest from sex and socialism

my molar needs a dentist
and my hamstring needs mending

the drip drop cadence of my leaky sink
reminds me I could use a nap from your eyes

www.ingramcontent.com/pod-product-compliance
Lightning Source LLC
LaVergne TN
LVHW091157080426
835509LV00006B/725